Edited by Claire Throp and John-Paul Wilkins

Designed by Tim Bond

Original illustrations © Capstone Global Library Ltd 2014

Picture research by Elizabeth Alexander

Production by Helen McCreath

Originated by Capstone Global Library Ltd

Printed and bound in China

ISBN 978-1-4846-0409-0 (hardcover)
ISBN 978-1-4846-0410-6 (paperback)
ISBN 978-1-4846-0412-0 (eBook PDF)
18 17 16 15 14
10 9 8 7 6 5 4 3 2 1

Library of Congress Cataloging-in-Publication Data
Cataloging-in-Publication data is available from the Library of Congress.

Acknowledgments
We would like to thank the following for permission to reproduce photographs: Shutterstock
1 – blue butterfly (© Sofiaworld), 2 – red apple (© Valentina Razumova), 3, 20 – basketball
(© Gencho Petkov), 4, 17 – purple and yellow flowers (© tr3gin), 5, 16 – green and purple
balloons (© nikkytok), 6 – fish (© serg_dibrova), 7 – banana (© Malyshev Maksim), 8, 14, 15, 18
– blue and orange balls (© Irina Rogova), 9 – pink balloon (© Ruslan Semichev), 10 – orange
flower (© andersphoto), 11 – blue butterfly (© Denis Vrublevski), 12, 13 – red and green buttons
(© Artter), 19 – pink flower (© MiVa). All body numbers 1–20, on all pages © Capstone Publishers
(Karon Dubke).

Cover photograph of body numbers reproduced with permission of
© Capstone Publishers (Karon Dubke).

Every effort has been made to contact copyright holders of material reproduced in this book.
Any omissions will be rectified in subsequent printings if notice is given to the publisher.

Number Fun

Making Numbers With Your Body

Isabel Thomas

Heinemann
LIBRARY

Chicago, Illinois

Are you ready for some number fun?

Do these things as you look through the book.

- Name the numbers that you see. Find them on the number line.

- Count the number of everyday objects in each picture.

- Find numbers made from straight lines and numbers made from curvy lines.

- Which numbers have straight lines and curvy lines?

- Trace the number shapes with your finger.

- Count the number of children in each picture.

- Name the parts of the body and the colors that you see. The list in the Picture Glossary will help you.

Can you make numbers with your body?

1 2 3 4 5 6 7 8 9 10 11 12 13 14 15 16 17 18 19 20

2

1 2 3 4 5 6 7 8 9 10 11 12 13 14 15 16 17 18 19 20

3

1 2 3 4 5 6 7 8 9 10 11 12 13 14 15 16 17 18 19 20

4

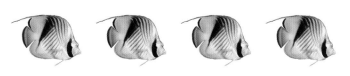

1 2 3 **4** 5 6 7 8 9 10 11 12 13 14 15 16 17 18 19 20

5

6

1 2 3 4 5 6 7 8 9 10 11 12 13 14 15 16 17 18 19 20

7

1 2 3 4 5 6 **7** 8 9 10 11 12 13 14 15 16 17 18 19 20

8

1 2 3 4 5 6 7 8 9 10 11 12 13 14 15 16 17 18 19 20

9

1 2 3 4 5 6 7 8 9 10 11 12 13 14 15 16 17 18 19 20

10

1 2 3 4 5 6 7 8 9 10 11 12 13 14 15 16 17 18 19 20

1 2 3 4 5 6 7 8 9 10 11 12 13 14 15 16 17 18 19 20

12

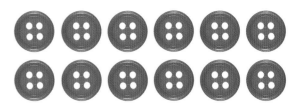

1 2 3 4 5 6 7 8 9 10 11 12 13 14 15 16 17 18 19 20

13

1 2 3 4 5 6 7 8 9 10 11 12 13 14 15 16 17 18 19 20

14

1 2 3 4 5 6 7 8 9 10 11 12 13 14 15 16 17 18 19 20

15

1 2 3 4 5 6 7 8 9 10 11 12 13 14 15 16 17 18 19 20

16

1 2 3 4 5 6 7 8 9 10 11 12 13 14 15 **16** 17 18 19 20

17

1 2 3 4 5 6 7 8 9 10 11 12 13 14 15 16 **17** 18 19 20

18

●●●●●●●●●
●●●●●●●●●

1 2 3 4 5 6 7 8 9 10 11 12 13 14 15 16 17 18 19 20

19

1 2 3 4 5 6 7 8 9 10 11 12 13 14 15 16 17 18 19 20

20

🏀 🏀 🏀 🏀 🏀 🏀 🏀 🏀 🏀 🏀
🏀 🏀 🏀 🏀 🏀 🏀 🏀 🏀 🏀 🏀

1 2 3 4 5 6 7 8 9 10 11 12 13 14 15 16 17 18 19 **20**

My Body: Picture Glossary

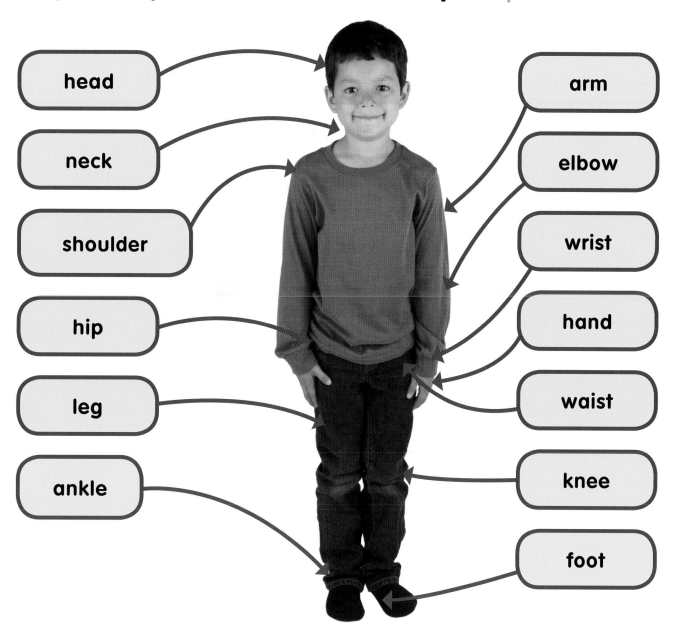

head

neck

shoulder

hip

leg

ankle

arm

elbow

wrist

hand

waist

knee

foot

Number Games

- **Number charades**. One pair or team forms a number with their bodies. The other teams have to guess the number which has been formed.

- **Musical numbers**. Play some music. When the music stops, players use their bodies to form the number called out. Make the game more difficult by asking players to form the number that comes before or after the number called out.

- **Count the steps**. Sit in a large circle. Challenge players one by one to walk, hop, or jump over to another player in a certain number of steps, counting aloud as they move. They can take that player's seat if they make the journey in the right number of steps. If they use too many or too few steps, they have to play again.

- **Tap and count**. Stand in a circle. One player starts by tapping a balloon toward another player and counting aloud: "one." The next player taps the balloon toward another player and counts aloud: "two." If someone drops the balloon, he or she is out and the counting restarts at "one." Continue until there are just two players left. Can the children tap and count all the way up to 100?

Notes for Parents and Teachers

There are lots of different ways to use *Number Fun* to practice number recognition and counting.

Young readers will enjoy looking at the photographs and talking about how each number is formed. Use the questions on page 3 to explore the book together. Encourage children to use positional language, such as *next to*, *under*, *on*, and *behind*.

Active learners will enjoy making number shapes using their own bodies.

They can use the ideas in the book or find new ways to make each number. Work in pairs or groups to form double-digit numbers. Games such as number shape charades and musical numbers will develop balance and coordination.

Take photographs of learners making numbers with their bodies. Compare these pictures with those in this book. Which numbers were easiest to make and why? You could print and display the photographs to make a fun, personalized number line.